# Challenging Poor Practice in Health and Social Care

# Care Practitioner Guide

HSC TRAINING LINK

# CONTENTS

# ACKNOWLEDGMENTS

Nursing and Midwifery Council. NMC:
https://www.nmc.org.uk/standards/code/read-the-code-online/
Care Quality Commission. CQC: https://www.cqc.org.uk/
Skills for Care: https://www.skillsforcare.org.uk/Support-for-leaders-and-managers/Managing-a-service/Safeguarding.aspx
SCIE:
https://www.scie.org.uk/dignity/care#:~:text=Dignity%20in%20care%20means%20providing,does%20nothing%20to%20undermine%20it
Dignity in Care:
https://www.dignityincare.org.uk/Resources/

# 1 INTRODUCTION

Challenging poor practice in adult social care settings is of paramount importance as it not only ensures the well-being and safety of vulnerable individuals but also upholds the fundamental principles of dignity, respect and human rights.

Taking a proactive stance against poor practice fosters a culture of accountability and continuous improvement within the care sector, enhancing the overall quality of care provided to those who rely on these services.

Addressing and rectifying poor practices can prevent potential harm, abuse and neglect and promote an environment where individuals can flourish and maintain their autonomy and independence.

Emphasising the significance of challenging poor practice reinforces the commitment to achieving the highest standards of care, promoting person-centered approaches and safeguarding the welfare of all service users.

**Important points:**

**Safeguarding Vulnerable Individuals:**

Challenging poor practice is crucial in safeguarding vulnerable adults who may be unable to advocate for themselves or identify substandard care. It ensures that their rights are protected and they are treated with dignity, respect and empathy throughout their care journey.

**Continuous Quality Improvement:**

By confronting poor practice, care providers can identify areas of improvement and implement necessary changes to enhance the overall quality of care.

This fosters a culture of learning and development, promoting best practices and innovation within the adult social care sector.

**Preventing Harm and Abuse:**

Addressing poor practice promptly can prevent potential harm, abuse and neglect experienced by vulnerable individuals.

It acts as a proactive measure to stop any detrimental behaviour and hold individuals or organisations accountable for their actions.

**Promoting Person-Centered Care:**

Challenging poor practice reinforces the importance of person-centered care, where the needs, preferences and aspirations of individuals are at the heart of decision-making.

By advocating for person-centered approaches, the care sector can ensure that service users' individuality and autonomy are respected, resulting in more tailored and effective care outcomes.

Social care staff have a duty of care to provide a range of acts of care to support and promote the well-being of the individuals they serve.

Here are some specific examples of these acts:

## Personal Care Assistance:

Social care staff may assist individuals with personal hygiene tasks, such as bathing, dressing, toileting and grooming, ensuring they maintain their dignity and personal well-being.

## Medication Management:

Staff should administer medications according to prescribed schedules, ensuring that individuals receive the correct dosage at the right time and maintain accurate records of medication administration.

## Nutrition and Meal Support:

Social care staff should provide appropriate meal planning and support individuals with eating, ensuring they receive proper nutrition and hydration as per their dietary needs and preferences.

## Mobility Support:

Staff may assist individuals with mobility challenges, helping them to move around safely, use mobility aids and perform exercises to maintain their physical independence.

## Social Engagement:

Social care staff should encourage and facilitate social interactions and engagement with others, ensuring that individuals remain connected with their community and combat feelings of isolation.

## Emotional Support:

Staff should provide emotional support and empathy to individuals, actively listening to their concerns, fears or anxieties and offering reassurance and comfort when needed.

## Health Monitoring:

Social care staff may monitor individuals' health conditions, reporting any changes or concerns to appropriate healthcare professionals to ensure timely and appropriate medical attention.

## Promoting Independence:

Staff should enable individuals to maintain as much independence as possible by supporting them in making their own choices, encouraging decision-making and fostering self-reliance.

## Safety and Risk Management:

Social care staff should create a safe environment by identifying and addressing potential hazards, implementing risk management strategies and ensuring individuals' safety at all times.

## Advocacy:

Staff may act as advocates for individuals, ensuring that their rights and preferences are respected and their needs are effectively communicated to relevant authorities and stakeholders.

**Personal Development:**

Social care staff may facilitate opportunities for personal development and learning, supporting individuals in pursuing their interests, hobbies and skills to enhance their overall well-being.

**End-of-Life Care:**

For those requiring end-of-life care, staff should provide compassionate and dignified support, addressing physical, emotional and spiritual needs while respecting the individual's wishes and cultural beliefs.

# 2 WHY CHALLENGE POOR PRACTICE?

Challenging poor practice in healthcare and social care is crucial for several reasons:

## 1. Patient/Client Safety:

The primary reason for challenging poor practice is to ensure the safety and well-being of patients and individuals receiving care.

Poor practice can lead to medical errors, injuries or neglect, which can have severe consequences for the health and safety of vulnerable individuals.

**Patient and client safety is a paramount concern in healthcare and social care settings.**

**Challenging poor practice is an essential component of safeguarding the safety and well-being of individuals in care.**

Here's more information on the importance of patient/client safety and how challenging poor practice plays a critical role:

**Preventing Medical Errors:**

Poor practice can encompass a range of issues, including medication errors, incorrect procedures, inadequate hygiene practices and more.

Challenging poor practice helps identify and rectify these errors before they harm patients or clients.

Medical errors can lead to adverse events, complications and even fatalities, making prevention a top priority.

**Avoiding Injuries:**

Inadequate care practices can result in physical injuries to patients or clients.

For example, improper lifting and handling techniques can cause musculoskeletal injuries to both caregivers and those in care.

Challenging and correcting these practices are vital to prevent injuries.

**Neglect Prevention:**

Neglect is a form of poor practice where individuals do not receive the necessary care and attention they require.

This can result in physical and psychological harm, deteriorating health conditions and a diminished quality of life.

Challenging neglectful behaviours or practices is essential for protecting individuals from such harm.

**Ensuring Dignity:**

Patients and clients have a right to receive care that respects their dignity and autonomy.

Poor practice that disregards these principles can lead to feelings of disrespect and degradation.

Challenging such practices is crucial for upholding the dignity of individuals in care.

**Building Trust:**

Patient/client trust in healthcare and social care providers is built on the assurance of safety.

When individuals know that their safety is a top priority, they are more likely to engage in care, follow treatment plans and communicate openly with healthcare professionals.

Challenging poor practice helps maintain and strengthen this trust.

## 2. Legal and Ethical Obligations:

Healthcare professionals have legal and ethical obligations to provide care that is safe and free from harm. Failing to challenge poor practice can result in legal liabilities and ethical violations.

In the United Kingdom, healthcare and care professionals are bound by a framework of laws, regulations and ethical principles that mandate the delivery of safe and high-quality care to patients and service users.

**Challenging poor practice is a crucial aspect of fulfilling these legal and ethical obligations.**

Here's more information on the legal and ethical considerations:

**Legal Obligations:**

**Duty of Care:**

Healthcare and care professionals have a legal duty of care towards their patients or clients.

This duty encompasses the responsibility to provide care that is safe, effective and in line with professional standards.

**Negligence:**

Failing to challenge and rectify poor practice can be construed as negligence. Negligence occurs when a healthcare or care professional breaches their duty of care, resulting in harm to the patient or client.

Negligence can lead to legal liability, including lawsuits and compensation claims.

**Regulatory Framework:**

Various regulatory bodies in the UK oversee healthcare and social care professions.

These bodies set standards of practice and conduct that professionals must adhere to.

Challenging poor practice is essential for complying with these regulatory requirements.

**Mandatory Reporting:**

In some cases, healthcare professionals are legally obligated to report poor practice or certain incidents, such as safeguarding concerns, to relevant authorities.

Failure to report can lead to legal consequences.

**Human Rights Act:**

The Human Rights Act 1998 incorporates the European Convention on Human Rights into UK law.

It ensures that individuals receiving care have certain rights, including the right to life, the prohibition of torture or inhuman treatment and the right to respect for private and family life.

Failing to challenge poor practice that violates these rights can result in legal challenges under this Act.

**Ethical Obligations:**

**Professional Codes of Conduct:**

Healthcare and care professions in the UK have their own codes of conduct and ethics.

These codes outline the ethical principles and standards that professionals must uphold.

Challenging poor practice is often explicitly mentioned as an ethical duty in these codes.

**Beneficence and Non-Maleficence:**

Two core ethical principles in healthcare are beneficence (doing good) and non-maleficence (do no harm).

Challenging poor practice aligns with these principles by promoting the well-being of patients and preventing harm.

**Patient/Client Autonomy:**

Respecting patient/client autonomy is another fundamental ethical principle.

This involves involving patients in decisions about their care. Challenging poor practice can ensure that patients' choices and preferences are respected.

**Accountability:**

Ethical professionalism includes being accountable for one's actions and decisions.

Challenging poor practice demonstrates accountability and a commitment to ethical practice.

**Advocacy:**

Advocating for patients or clients is an ethical duty.

This includes speaking up against poor practice and ensuring that individuals receive the best possible care.

**Whistleblowing:**

Ethical considerations also encompass whistleblowing when necessary.

Whistleblowing is the act of reporting serious concerns about practices that may harm patients or the public.

It is viewed as an ethical duty to protect the welfare of individuals receiving care.

**Quality Improvement:**

Challenging poor practice is not just about preventing harm; it is also about improving the quality of care.

Identifying and rectifying substandard practices contribute to a culture of continuous improvement in healthcare and social care organisations.

**Patient Advocacy:**

Healthcare professionals often act as advocates for their patients or clients.

Advocacy includes challenging poor practice and ensuring that individuals receive the best possible care.

It involves speaking up on behalf of those who may be unable to do so for themselves.

**Regulatory Compliance:**

Healthcare organisations are subject to regulations and standards that require them to provide safe and effective care.

Challenging poor practice is necessary for compliance with these regulations and to maintain accreditation and licensing.

**Quality of Care:**

Challenging poor practice is essential for maintaining high standards of care.

It helps prevent substandard care from becoming the norm and promotes a culture of continuous improvement in healthcare and social care settings.

# 3. Professional Integrity:

Challenging poor practice upholds the professional integrity and reputation of healthcare and social care workers.

It demonstrates a commitment to ethical standards and the well-being of patients.

**Here's more information on the professional integrity considerations:**

**Trust and Confidence:**

The trust and confidence of patients, clients and the public are paramount in healthcare and social care professions.

Challenging poor practice when encountered sends a clear message that professionals prioritise the well-being and safety of those they serve.

This commitment to ethical practice enhances trust and confidence in the profession.

## Maintaining Standards:

Healthcare and social care professions have established standards of practice and ethical codes that guide their members.

Challenging poor practice is consistent with these standards and demonstrates a commitment to upholding them.

This adherence to professional standards is vital for maintaining the integrity of the profession.

## Accountability:

Part of professional integrity involves being accountable for one's actions and decisions.

When professionals challenge poor practice, they accept accountability for the quality of care they provide.

This accountability fosters transparency and a sense of responsibility.

## Respect for Patients'/Clients' Rights:

Upholding professional integrity means respecting the rights and dignity of patients or clients.

Challenging poor practice ensures that patients' rights to safe and ethical care are protected.

This respect for individual rights contributes to a positive professional reputation.

## Ethical Reputation:

Healthcare and social care professions have strong ethical foundations.

Challenging poor practice aligns with these ethical principles and reinforces the profession's reputation for ethical conduct.

## Learning and Improvement:

Challenging poor practice also reflects a commitment to continuous learning and improvement.

It acknowledges that professionals are open to feedback, willing to learn from mistakes and dedicated to enhancing the quality of care they provide.

## Peer Recognition:

Within the healthcare and social care community, professionals who consistently challenge and address poor practice are often recognised and respected by their peers.

They are seen as advocates for patient safety and champions of ethical practice.

## Legal and Ethical Obligations:

As discussed earlier, professionals have legal and ethical obligations to challenge poor practice.

Fulfilling these obligations is not only a matter of compliance but also a reflection of their commitment to professional integrity.

## 4. Preventing Harm:

Poor practice can result in harm to patients/clients, including physical, emotional or psychological harm.

Challenging such practice is essential for preventing harm and ensuring that individuals receive the care they deserve.

**Here's more information on preventing harm considerations:**

**Physical Harm:**

Poor practice can directly lead to physical harm to patients or clients.

This harm may manifest as injuries, complications or worsening of existing medical conditions.

For example, administering the wrong medication dosage can result in physical harm, such as adverse reactions or treatment ineffectiveness.

**Emotional and Psychological Harm:**

Poor practice can also cause emotional and psychological harm.

Patients or clients may experience distress, anxiety or trauma when subjected to neglect, disrespect or unprofessional behaviour.

Emotional harm can have long-lasting effects on mental well-being.

**Dignity and Respect:**

Every individual receiving care has the right to be treated with dignity and respect.

Poor practice that compromises this dignity by, for example, disregarding privacy or using demeaning language can cause significant emotional harm.

Challenging such practices helps protect the dignity of those in care.

## Quality of Life:

Preventing harm is not only about avoiding physical injuries but also about improving the overall quality of life for patients or clients.

Poor practice can hinder individuals' recovery, rehabilitation or enjoyment of life.

Challenging such practices ensures that care contributes positively to well-being.

## Long-Term Consequences:

Harm caused by poor practice can have long-term consequences.

This may result in extended hospital stays, increased healthcare costs and a reduced quality of life.

Preventing harm through vigilant practice and timely challenges can mitigate these negative outcomes.

## Patient/Client Trust:

Patients and clients place their trust in healthcare and social care professionals.

When harm occurs due to poor practice, this trust is eroded.

Challenging poor practice not only prevents harm but also helps maintain and rebuild trust with those under care.

## Ethical Responsibility:

Healthcare and social care professionals have an ethical responsibility to prioritise the well-being and safety of their patients or clients.

Challenging poor practice is an ethical imperative rooted in the principle of beneficence, which requires professionals to act in the best interests of those they serve.

**Regulatory Compliance:**

In many healthcare systems, there are regulatory requirements and standards aimed at preventing harm.

Challenging poor practice is a means of ensuring compliance with these regulations, which are designed to safeguard patients and clients.

**Continuous Improvement:**

By challenging poor practice, professionals contribute to a culture of continuous improvement in healthcare and social care settings.

Identifying and rectifying issues that lead to harm can lead to better care practices and ultimately enhance the quality of care provided.

**Advocacy:**

Challenging poor practice often involves advocating for the rights and well-being of patients or clients.

This advocacy role is central to preventing harm and ensuring that individuals receive care that meets their needs and respects their rights.

## 5. Continuous Improvement:

By challenging poor practice, healthcare organisations and professionals can identify areas for improvement.

This feedback loop allows for the implementation of changes and enhancements to healthcare processes and practices.

**Here's more information on continuous improvement considerations:**

**Identifying Weaknesses:**

Challenging poor practice involves critically assessing current healthcare processes and practices.

It often reveals weaknesses, inefficiencies and areas where improvement is needed.

These identified weaknesses become the starting point for meaningful change.

**Data-Driven Decision Making:**

Challenging poor practice is based on evidence and data.

When healthcare professionals identify and report instances of poor practice, they provide valuable data that can be used for analysis.

This data-driven approach enables organisations to make informed decisions about where improvements are most urgently needed.

**Root Cause Analysis:**

Challenging poor practice often involves conducting root cause analyses to understand why the poor practice occurred in the first place.

This in-depth examination helps organisations pinpoint underlying issues or systemic problems contributing to suboptimal care.

Addressing root causes is essential for sustainable improvement.

## Quality Assurance:

Continuous improvement in healthcare is closely tied to quality assurance efforts.

By addressing poor practice, healthcare organisations can enhance the quality of care delivered to patients.

This includes measures to ensure that care is safe, effective, patient-centred, timely, efficient and equitable, as defined by the Institute of Medicine's quality aims.

## Enhancing Patient/Client Safety:

A key aspect of continuous improvement is enhancing patient safety.

Poor practice can pose significant risks to patient safety. Identifying and addressing these risks through challenging poor practice is integral to creating safer healthcare environments.

## Process Optimisation:

Challenging poor practice often leads to process optimisation.

When professionals and organisations recognise areas of inefficiency or bottlenecks contributing to poor practice, they can redesign processes to streamline workflows, reduce errors and improve overall efficiency.

## Training and Education:

Identifying instances of poor practice can highlight gaps in the knowledge and skills of healthcare professionals.

This insight can lead to targeted training and education programs to ensure that all staff members are well-equipped to provide high-quality care.

**Feedback Loops:**

Challenging poor practice creates feedback loops within healthcare organisations.

This means that frontline staff are actively engaged in identifying problems and suggesting solutions.

Organisations that value and act on this feedback tend to be more responsive to changing needs and better positioned for improvement.

**Patient/Client-Centred Care:**
 Continuous improvement efforts often prioritise patient-centred care.

Challenging poor practice that compromises patient-centredness can lead to initiatives that prioritise individual preferences, involve patients in decision-making and improve communication between healthcare providers and patients.

**Accreditation and Certification:**

Many healthcare organisations seek accreditation and certification from external bodies.

Challenging poor practice and demonstrating a commitment to continuous improvement are essential for maintaining and achieving these credentials, which can boost an organisation's reputation and funding.

## 6. Accountability:

Challenging poor practice holds individuals and organisations accountable for their actions.

It ensures that those responsible for substandard care are

appropriately addressed and that systemic issues are addressed to prevent future occurrences.

**Here's more information on accountability considerations:**

**Individual Responsibility:**

Challenging poor practice places a spotlight on individual responsibility within healthcare.

It reminds healthcare professionals that they have a duty to provide safe and effective care to their patients or clients.

When poor practice is identified, individuals responsible can be held accountable for their actions.

**Organisational Accountability:**

Healthcare organisations also bear a significant responsibility for the care they provide.

Challenging poor practice encourages organisations to take ownership of systemic issues that may contribute to substandard care.

This includes addressing problems within their policies, procedures and culture.

**Transparency:**

Accountability promotes transparency in healthcare.

When poor practice is challenged, it often involves open and honest communication about what went wrong and why.

This transparency can help patients, their families and the public understand what happened and what measures are being taken to prevent recurrence.

**Learning from Mistakes:**

Accountability is closely tied to learning from mistakes.

In healthcare, as in any field, errors can occur.

Challenging poor practice creates opportunities for individuals and organisations to learn from their mistakes.

This can lead to improvements in processes and practices to prevent similar errors in the future.

**Professional Standards:**

Healthcare professionals are bound by ethical and professional standards.

Challenging poor practice reinforces the importance of adhering to these standards.

It sends a message that deviation from established norms is not acceptable and can have consequences.

**Quality Improvement:**

Accountability is a driver for quality improvement.

When poor practice is identified, it prompts organisations to evaluate their quality improvement measures.

This can lead to the implementation of new protocols, training programs and monitoring systems to enhance the overall quality of care.

**Patient/Client Trust:**

Accountability is crucial for building and maintaining patient trust.

When patients or clients see that healthcare organisations and professionals take responsibility for their actions and work to improve, it fosters trust.

Trust is a fundamental component of the patient-provider relationship.

**Regulatory Compliance:**

Many healthcare organisations must comply with regulatory requirements.

Challenging poor practice ensures that these requirements are met.

It can also result in corrective actions to address deficiencies and prevent regulatory violations.

**Ethical Considerations:**

Healthcare is governed by a strong ethical framework.

Accountability aligns with ethical principles such as beneficence (doing good) and non-maleficence (doing no harm).

Challenging poor practice underscores the ethical duty to provide the best possible care.

**Preventing Recurrence:**

Ultimately, accountability is about preventing the recurrence of poor practice.

When individuals and organisations take responsibility for their actions, they are motivated to make the necessary changes to prevent similar incidents in the future.

This proactive approach contributes to a safer and more effective healthcare system.

## 7. Trust and Confidence:

Patients/clients and their families place their trust and confidence in healthcare and social care professionals.

Challenging poor practice helps maintain and build trust by demonstrating a commitment to providing the best possible care.

**Here's more information on trust and confidence considerations:**

**Patient/Client-Centred Care:**
 Challenging poor practice reinforces the commitment of healthcare and social care professionals to patient-centred care.

Patients/clients and their families place their trust in the hands of these professionals, expecting that their well-being and safety will be the top priority.

When poor practice is identified and addressed, it sends a clear message that patient safety and quality care are paramount.

**Transparency:**

Trust is built on transparency and open communication.

Challenging poor practice often involves candid discussions about what went wrong and why.

This transparency is crucial in maintaining trust, as it shows that healthcare professionals are willing to admit mistakes and take corrective action.

Patients/clients and their families are more likely to trust providers who are open about their actions.

**Accountability:**

Trust is closely tied to accountability.

When poor practice is challenged, it holds individuals and organisations accountable for their actions.

Patients and their families expect that healthcare providers will be accountable for the care they deliver.

Knowing that accountability exists reinforces trust in the healthcare system.

## Quality Assurance:

Trust is also linked to the assurance of quality care. Patients/clients and their families want to know that they will receive high-quality care that meets established standards.

Challenging poor practice is a way to ensure that quality standards are upheld.

Patients/clients can have confidence in the care they receive when they see that deviations from these standards are addressed promptly.

## Confidence in Decision-Making:

Patients/clients and their families often rely on the expertise of healthcare professionals when making important medical decisions.

Trust in these professionals' competence and judgment is crucial.

Challenging poor practice demonstrates a commitment to making informed, evidence-based decisions, which enhances patients' confidence in the care they receive.

## Preventing Harm:

Trust is closely connected to the prevention of harm.

Patients/clients trust that healthcare providers will do no harm and will take all necessary precautions to protect their well-being.

Challenging poor practice is a proactive measure to prevent harm, reinforcing patients' confidence in the safety of their care.

## Emotional Support:

Trust is not limited to clinical competence. It also extends to emotional support.

Patients/clients and their families expect that healthcare professionals will show empathy and compassion.

Challenging poor practice includes providing emotional support to those affected by substandard care, which can rebuild trust and confidence.

## Patient/Client-Caregiver Relationship:

The patient-caregiver relationship is built on trust.

Patients must have confidence in their healthcare providers to share sensitive information and make collaborative decisions.

Challenging poor practice contributes to maintaining a positive patient-caregiver relationship by demonstrating a commitment to addressing concerns and providing safe care.

## Shared Decision-Making:

Trust is essential for shared decision-making.

Patients/clients and their families want to be active participants in their care.

Challenging poor practice promotes a culture of shared decision-making, where patients/clients and providers work together to determine the best course of action.

## Overall Satisfaction:

Trust and confidence significantly influence overall satisfaction with healthcare services.

When patients and their families have trust and confidence in their healthcare providers, they are more likely to be satisfied with their care experience.

## 8. Regulatory Compliance:

Healthcare organisations are often subject to regulations and standards that require them to maintain certain levels of care quality.

Challenging poor practice is necessary for compliance with these regulations and to avoid legal repercussions.

**Here's more information on regulatory compliance considerations:**

**Legal Requirements:**

Challenging poor practice is essential to meet legal requirements and obligations.

Healthcare and social care organisations and professionals are bound by various laws and regulations that mandate the delivery of safe and high-quality care.

When poor practice is identified and addressed promptly, it helps ensure compliance with these legal standards.

**Patient Safety Regulations:**

Many healthcare regulations are specifically designed to protect patient safety.

Challenging poor practice is a proactive step to adhere to regulations related to patient safety.

It demonstrates a commitment to upholding these

regulations and preventing harm to patients.

## Accreditation Standards:

Healthcare organisations often seek accreditation from accrediting bodies and agencies.

These accrediting bodies establish specific standards for care quality and safety.

Challenging poor practice is crucial for maintaining accreditation status, as deviations from these standards can lead to accreditation loss.

## Quality Improvement:

Regulatory compliance is closely linked to quality improvement efforts.

Challenging poor practice is a means of continuous quality improvement.

Healthcare and social care organisations that actively address and rectify areas of poor practice demonstrate their commitment to enhancing the quality of care they provide.

## Risk Management:

Effective risk management is a fundamental component of regulatory compliance.

Challenging poor practice helps identify risks and vulnerabilities within healthcare processes.

By addressing these issues, organisations mitigate the risk of legal consequences resulting from poor practice.

## Data Reporting:

In many healthcare systems, data reporting is required to

monitor and assess care quality.

Challenging poor practice may involve collecting and reporting data on adverse events or incidents related to substandard care.

Accurate data reporting is vital for compliance with regulatory requirements.

## Accountability:

Regulatory compliance often involves accountability for care quality.

Challenging poor practice holds individuals and organisations accountable for deviations from established standards.

This accountability aligns with the expectations set by regulatory bodies.

Patient/Client Rights:

Regulations frequently outline the rights of patients, including the right to receive safe and appropriate care.

Challenging poor practice is consistent with protecting and upholding these patient rights, ensuring that individuals receive the care to which they are entitled.

## Documentation and Record-Keeping:

Regulatory compliance often includes stringent requirements for documentation and record-keeping.

Challenging poor practice may involve maintaining detailed records of incidents, investigations and actions taken to address substandard care.

Proper documentation is critical for demonstrating compliance.

## Inspections and Audits:

Healthcare and social care organisations will undergo inspections and audits by regulatory authorities.

Challenging poor practice proactively prepares organisations for such inspections.

When regulatory authorities find that an organisation actively addresses and rectifies poor practice, it reflects positively on compliance efforts.

**Here are some of the key regulations and standards relevant to healthcare and social care:**

### Care Quality Commission (CQC):

The CQC is the independent regulator of health and social care services in England.

It monitors, inspects and regulates care providers to ensure they meet essential standards of quality and safety.

Organisations must comply with CQC standards to operate legally.

### Health and Social Care Act 2008 (Regulated Activities) Regulations:

These regulations set out the legal framework for the registration and regulation of healthcare and social care providers in England.

They define the regulated activities that require registration with the CQC.

### National Health Service (NHS) Constitution:

The NHS Constitution sets out the rights and responsibilities of patients and staff within the NHS in England.

It includes principles and values that underpin healthcare delivery, such as the right to high-quality care.

**The Fundamental Standards:**

The CQC's Fundamental Standards represent the basic standards of care that all providers must meet.

These standards cover areas such as dignity and respect, consent, safety and cleanliness.

**Mental Capacity Act 2005:**

This legislation provides a legal framework for making decisions on behalf of individuals who may lack the capacity to make decisions themselves.

It sets out principles for decision-making and safeguards to protect vulnerable individuals.

**Health and Safety at Work Act 1974:**

This Act places duties on employers to ensure the health, safety and well-being of their employees and others who may be affected by their work activities.

It includes provisions related to risk assessment and safe working practices.

**Data Protection Act 2018 and General Data Protection Regulation (GDPR):**

These regulations govern the processing of personal data, including patient and service user information.

Healthcare and social care organisations must comply with strict data protection requirements to safeguard individuals' privacy and confidentiality.

**The Mental Health Act 1983 (as amended in 2007):**

This legislation provides the legal framework for the detention and treatment of individuals with mental health disorders. It includes safeguards to protect patients' rights and well-being.

**Human Rights Act 1998:**

This Act incorporates the European Convention on Human Rights into UK law.

It sets out fundamental human rights and freedoms, including the right to life, freedom from torture and the right to respect for private and family life.

**National Institute for Health and Care Excellence (NICE) Guidelines:**

NICE provides evidence-based guidelines and recommendations for healthcare and social care practice.

While not legally binding, these guidelines are influential in shaping care standards and best practices.

**Social Care Wales and Care Inspectorate Wales:**

In Wales, these bodies regulate and inspect social care services. They set standards and ensure compliance with regulations.

**Scottish Social Services Council (SSSC) and Care Inspectorate (Scotland):**

In Scotland, the SSSC is responsible for regulating and registering social service workers, while the Care Inspectorate inspects and regulates care services.

**Regulation and Quality Improvement Authority (RQIA) (Northern Ireland):**

RQIA regulates and inspects health and social care services in Northern Ireland.

# 9. Ethical Duty to Report:

Healthcare professionals have an ethical duty to report poor practice when they witness it.

Failing to report can be seen as condoning or enabling poor care, which is inconsistent with the ethical principles of healthcare.

**Here's more information on ethical duty to report considerations:**

**Beneficence:**

Beneficence is an ethical principle that underscores the obligation of healthcare and social care professionals to act in the best interests of their patients or service users.

Reporting poor practice is an essential aspect of beneficence because it aims to protect individuals from harm and ensure they receive the best possible care.

**Non-Maleficence:**

Non-maleficence is the principle of "do no harm."

Reporting poor practice is a way to prevent or mitigate harm that may result from substandard care.

By reporting, professionals are actively working to minimise the potential harm caused by poor practice.

**Justice:**

The principle of justice emphasises fairness and the equitable distribution of resources and care.

Reporting poor practice is essential for upholding justice in healthcare and social care settings because it helps ensure that all individuals, regardless of their circumstances, receive high-quality care and are protected from harm.

**Autonomy:**

Autonomy refers to an individual's right to make informed decisions about their own care and well-being.

When professionals report poor practice, they support the autonomy of patients and service users by advocating for care that respects their preferences and rights.

**Veracity:**

Veracity is the principle of truthfulness and honesty.

Reporting poor practice aligns with veracity because it involves providing accurate and truthful information about situations where care falls short of expected standards.

It promotes transparency and accountability.

**Professional Codes of Ethics:**

Many healthcare and social care professions have established codes of ethics or conduct that explicitly require professionals to report unethical or poor practice.

These codes serve as guidelines for ethical behaviour and reinforce the duty to report.

**Patient/Client Advocacy:**

Healthcare and social care professionals often act as advocates for their patients or service users.

Reporting poor practice is a critical form of advocacy that ensures individuals receive safe and appropriate care and their rights are upheld.

## Organisational Accountability:

Professionals have an ethical obligation to hold their organisations accountable for providing safe and high-quality care.

Reporting poor practice is a way to address systemic issues and promote organisational accountability for the well-being of patients and service users.

## Professional Integrity:

Maintaining professional integrity and credibility is vital In healthcare and social care.

Reporting poor practice demonstrates a commitment to upholding ethical standards and professional integrity, which is essential for public trust and confidence.

## Preventing Recurrence:

Reporting poor practice is not just about addressing current issues; it's also about preventing future occurrences.

By reporting, professionals contribute to the improvement of care practices and help prevent similar problems from arising in the future.

**Challenging poor practice in healthcare and social care is imperative.**

**It safeguards the well-being and safety of individuals receiving care, upholds ethical obligations and maintains professional integrity.**

**By reporting and addressing substandard care, we**

prevent harm, promote continuous improvement and hold both individuals and organisations accountable for their actions.

Ultimately, challenging poor practice is a fundamental ethical duty that ensures the highest standards of care are consistently met.

# 3 SAFEGUARDING, DUTY OF CARE, MINDSET, ABUSE, POOR PRACTICE

Challenging poor practice is crucial in safeguarding vulnerable adults who may be unable to advocate for themselves or identify substandard care.

It ensures that their rights are protected and they are treated with dignity, respect and empathy.

## Addressing poor practice promptly:

- Can prevent potential harm, abuse and neglect experienced by vulnerable individuals.

- It acts as a proactive measure to stop any detrimental behaviour and hold individuals or organisations accountable for their actions.

## Promoting Person-Centred Care

Challenging poor practice reinforces the importance of person-centered care:

- Where the needs, preferences and aspirations of individuals are at the heart of all care provision

By advocating for person-centered approaches, the care sector can ensure that service users' individuality and autonomy are respected, resulting in more tailored and effective care outcomes.

## Can I Really Make a Difference?

Yes you can.

Challenging poor practice can be or seem quite daunting but if you see something or hear something that does not meet the standard of care that people are entitled to receive, you have a duty of care to do something about it

## What is the Duty of Care?

A Duty of care, in any setting, is the level of service that is expected (as a minimum) to be provided.

In health care and social care, this includes:

- Act in the best interests of individuals.

- Do not act or fail to act in a way that could cause harm.

- Always act within your own competence and do not do something which you can not do safely.

Health and social care staff have a duty of care to provide a range of acts of care to support and promote the well-being of the individuals they serve – including:

- Personal care assistance and medication management
- Nutrition and meal support and mobility support
- Social engagement and emotional support
- Health monitoring and promoting independence
- Safety and risk management and advocacy
- Personal development and end-of-life care

Duty of care in challenging poor practice is a fundamental ethical and professional obligation for healthcare and social care workers. It entails the responsibility to take all reasonable steps to ensure the safety, well-being and dignity of individuals in their care.

**When challenging poor practice, professionals must consider the following:**

1. **Patient-Centred Approach: The primary focus should always be on the best interests of the patient or client.**
   The duty of care requires professionals to act in a manner that prioritises the welfare of those receiving care.

2. **Ethical Considerations:** Challenging poor practice aligns with ethical principles such as beneficence (doing good) and non-maleficence (do no harm). It reflects a commitment to providing the highest quality care.

3. **Legal Obligations:** Many healthcare and social care workers are bound by legal obligations to report and address poor practice. Failure to do so may result in legal consequences, including negligence claims.

4. **Confidentiality:** While challenging poor practice, professionals must also respect the confidentiality and privacy of individuals involved. Information sharing should be limited to those directly responsible for addressing the issue.

5. **Support Systems:** Healthcare and social care organisations should have mechanisms in place to support employees in challenging poor practice. This

includes providing guidance, protection from retaliation and a clear reporting process.

6. **Documentation:** Professionals should maintain accurate records of incidents and their responses. This documentation serves as evidence of their commitment to duty of care and due diligence.

In summary, duty of care in challenging poor practice involves acting in the best interests of individuals receiving care, upholding ethical and legal responsibilities, maintaining confidentiality and using established support systems to address issues effectively while documenting the process for accountability.

## Working Poorly to 'Fit In'

Challenging poor practice isn't just about looking at others, procedures or service given.

You may find yourself in a situation where there is so much poor practice taking place that you feel pressured to change the way you work in order to fit in with the working environment and your colleagues.

Always maintain your own good practice .... you have a duty of care.

## Good Practice

The most simple explanation of good practice is providing high-quality, compassionate and safe care that meets the individual needs and preferences of each person receiving care.

It involves treating people with dignity and respect, promoting their well-being and following established guidelines and standards to ensure health and welfare is prioritised.

Good practice also includes effective communication, teamwork and continuous improvement to deliver the best possible care.

## Poor Practice

The most simple explanation of poor practice is failing to provide adequate, safe and respectful care to individuals.

It involves neglecting needs, not following established guidelines and standards, treating people without dignity and respect and not prioritising well-being.

Poor practice also includes ineffective communication, lack of teamwork and a failure to learn from mistakes or improve the quality of care provided.

Poor practice generally means that the needs of the person being cared for are not seen as important.

When such situations occur, the quality of care can deteriorate, perhaps becoming hasty, inconsistent and unreliable.

This deterioration can create an environment where individuals may be subject to mistreatment and lack of attention.

Consequently, the person receiving care may have a negative or deeply troubling experience.

Some instances of poor practice can be characterised as lacking effort, inconsiderate or careless.

They encompass actions that can be halted immediately if the caregiver recognises their behaviour and contemplates the impact it has on the person being assisted.

For instance, it might involve urging someone to take the lift because it's faster than using the stairs or engaging in personal phone calls when one-on-one support should be the focus.

## Witnessing Poor Practice

### Mindset

- If you have witnessed poor practice, how do you view it?
- What initially goes through your mind?
- Do you think that is is 'thoughtless or sloppy' or do you reflect on whether it is abusive?
- What sort of a mindset do you have?

You should always look at poor practice as an opportunity to change something for the better.

People's mindsets when witnessing or ignoring poor practice in healthcare and social care can be influenced by various factors, including personal beliefs, professional ethics, organisational culture and fear of repercussions.

**Here's a closer look at some common mindsets:**

**Ethical Mindset:**

Professionals with a strong ethical mindset prioritise patient well-being and are more likely to challenge poor practice.

They view their duty of care as a moral obligation and are guided by principles such as beneficence and non-maleficence.

## Fear and Reluctance:

Some individuals may witness poor practice but hesitate to intervene due to fear of consequences.

This fear could include concerns about retaliation, damage to their professional reputation or potential conflicts with colleagues or supervisors.

## Bystander Effect:

The bystander effect is a psychological phenomenon in which individuals are less likely to intervene when they believe others are present to address the issue.

In healthcare settings, this can lead to inaction when multiple people witness poor practice, assuming someone else will take responsibility.

## Compliance Mindset:

In highly hierarchical or authoritarian environments, individuals may adopt a compliance mindset.

They may follow orders or organisational norms without questioning them, even when they suspect poor practice.

This can result from a perceived lack of autonomy or fear of challenging authority.

## Cognitive Dissonance:

People experiencing cognitive dissonance may witness poor practice but attempt to rationalise it to reduce psychological discomfort.

They may convince themselves that the situation is not as bad as it seems or that someone else will handle it.

### Whistleblower Mindset:

Professionals who choose to report poor practice often have a whistleblower mindset.

They are willing to endure personal and professional risks to protect patient safety and uphold ethical standards. They see themselves as advocates for those receiving care.

### Organisational Culture:

The culture within a healthcare or social care organisation can significantly influence individuals' mindsets.

A culture that prioritises patient safety and encourages open communication is more likely to foster a mindset of challenging poor practice.

### Empowerment:

Feeling empowered within one's role can lead to a proactive mindset.

Empowered professionals believe they have the authority and responsibility to challenge and address poor practice, even if it means confronting colleagues or supervisors.

### Professional Identity:

A strong professional identity can shape one's mindset.

Those who strongly identify with their healthcare or social care profession may be more committed to ethical standards and patient well-being, making them more likely to challenge poor practice.

It's important to recognise that people's mindsets can evolve over time and may be influenced by education, training and workplace experiences.

Encouraging a culture that supports open communication,

ethical behaviour and reporting mechanisms can help shape positive mindsets that prioritise patient safety and the highest standards of care.

## Abuse

Abuse can take many forms and can include:

- Physical abuse
- Sexual abuse
- Psychological or emotional abuse
- Financial or material abuse
- Neglect
- Discriminatory abuse
- Institutional abuse

**If you witness poor practice that you believe to be abusive you need to consider the most appropriate way to deal with it.**

Abuse and poor practice in healthcare and social care are deeply concerning issues that can have severe consequences for individuals receiving care.

While they are **distinct problems**, there can be a **relationship** between them.

**Here's an overview of abuse, poor practice and their connection:**

**Abuse:** Abuse refers to the deliberate mistreatment, harm or exploitation of vulnerable individuals, often in a care giving or institutional setting.

It can take various forms, including:

1. **Physical Abuse:**

- This involves physical harm or force, such as hitting, slapping or restraining an individual, resulting in injury or pain.

2. **Emotional or Psychological Abuse:**

- Emotional abuse encompasses behaviours that cause emotional distress, such as intimidation, humiliation, isolation or verbal threats.

3. **Sexual Abuse:**

- Sexual abuse involves non-consensual sexual activities or exploitation, which is a gross violation of an individual's rights and dignity.

4. **Neglect:**

- Neglect is a form of abuse where caregivers fail to provide the necessary care, including basics like food, shelter and medical attention, leading to harm or suffering.

5. **Financial Exploitation:**

- Financial abuse entails the unauthorised or improper use of an individual's assets or finances, often for the abuser's benefit.

**Poor Practice:** Poor practice, on the other hand, involves a range of substandard or inadequate actions, behaviours or decisions by healthcare or social care professionals.

While poor practice may not always be intentional, it can still result in harm or inadequate care for patients or individuals receiving support.

Examples of poor practice include:

1. **Failure to Follow Protocols:**

- Healthcare providers not adhering to established protocols and standards of care, leading to medical errors or suboptimal treatment.

2. **Lack of Compassion and Communication:**

- Poor communication skills, lack of empathy or failure to involve patients or clients in decision-making can negatively affect the care experience.

3. **Inadequate Monitoring:**

- Not adequately monitoring patients' conditions, failing to report changes or not responding promptly to warning signs can lead to health deterioration.

4. **Medication Errors:**

- Administering the wrong medication, incorrect dosage or failing to document medication administration accurately can result in serious harm.

**Connection between Abuse and Poor Practice:**

There is a critical connection between abuse and poor practice in healthcare and social care settings:

1. **Failure to Prevent and Report Abuse:**

- Poor practice may involve failing to recognise and report signs of abuse, allowing abusive behaviour to persist.

- This can occur when staff members ignore or minimise abuse allegations or do not follow proper reporting procedures.

2. **Contributing Factors:**

- Some instances of abuse can be linked to systemic issues, such as inadequate staffing levels, poor training or a culture that tolerates neglect or mistreatment.

- These factors can create an environment conducive to both poor practice and abuse.

3. **Impact on Vulnerable Individuals:**

- Both abuse and poor practice can harm vulnerable individuals physically, emotionally and psychologically.

- Individuals may experience trauma, loss of trust and a decline in their overall well-being.

Addressing and preventing abuse and poor practice requires a multifaceted approach that includes robust reporting mechanisms, staff training, clear policies and a culture of accountability.

Healthcare and social care organisations must prioritise patient or client safety and well-being, fostering an environment where abuse and poor practice are not tolerated and individuals are treated with dignity and respect.

# 4 OBSERVED POOR PRACTICE?

If you've ever:

- Experienced unease about the level of care provided to an individual.
- Are aware that they deserved a more dignified and improved experience.

You have probably observed poor practices in action.

## Assessing the Situation

Assessing the situation when you suspect or observe poor practice in healthcare or social care is a crucial step in addressing and rectifying the issue.

**Here are some key aspects to consider when assessing such situations:**

## Gather Information:

Start by collecting as much information as possible about the situation.

This may include specific details of what you observed, the individuals involved, the date, time and location of the incident and any witnesses present.

## Trust Your Instincts:

Trust your gut feeling or intuition.

If something doesn't seem right, it's essential to take it seriously and investigate further.

Your instincts can be a valuable early warning system for identifying poor practice.

### Objectivity:

Try to maintain objectivity and avoid making assumptions or jumping to conclusions.

Keep an open mind and focus on facts and evidence.

### Consider the Impact:

Think about the potential consequences of the observed poor practice on the individuals receiving care.

Consider both immediate and long-term effects on their physical and emotional well-being.

### Consult Policies and Procedures:

Review the policies and procedures of your healthcare or social care organisation.

These guidelines often provide clear instructions on how to address and report poor practice.

Ensure you understand your role and responsibilities in such situations.

### Speak with Colleagues:

If you're comfortable, discuss your concerns with trusted colleagues who may have witnessed the same situation.

They can provide additional insights and support your assessment of the situation.

## Document:

Document your observations and concerns in writing. Include all relevant details, such as dates, times, locations and the people involved.

This documentation can be valuable if you need to report the issue formally.

## Assess the Severity:

Evaluate the severity of the poor practice. Is it an isolated incident or does it appear to be part of a pattern of behaviour?

Determine if immediate action is required or if it's a matter that can be addressed through less urgent means.

## Determine Reporting Channels:

Identify the appropriate channels for reporting poor practice within your organisation.

This may involve reporting to a supervisor, manager or an internal reporting system.

Understand the process and follow it accordingly.

## Seek Guidance:

If you're unsure about how to proceed or if you have concerns about potential retaliation, seek guidance from a trusted mentor, a professional association or an independent advocacy group.

They can offer advice and support.

## Maintain Confidentiality:

Respect the privacy and confidentiality of all individuals involved.

Avoid discussing the situation with anyone not directly involved in addressing it.

**Be Prepared for Resistance:**

In some cases, you may encounter resistance or pushback when addressing poor practice.

Be prepared to persist in advocating for the best interests of the individuals receiving care.

**Assessing the situation is a critical first step in addressing poor practice effectively.**

It allows you to gather information, evaluate the impact and determine the appropriate course of action, all with the goal of ensuring the safety, dignity and well-being of those under your care.

**When assessing the situation, consider the following questions:**

1. Carefully assess the situation and think about what you've seen or heard.

2. How do you feel, what is your instinct telling you?

3. Have you considered all possibilities – perhaps things aren't as they first appeared.

4. Explore your options.

5. What action is most appropriate?

6. Is it feasible to challenge right away whilst the act is taking place?

7. Or do you need to speak to your manager or another senior manager or implement the whistleblowing policy?

8. Can it wait or do you need to do something straight away?

**If the person is in immediate danger (physical or mental) then you need to act instantly.**

- Tell your manager or another senior manager.

- Keep the person at the centre – don't lose sight of their needs and feelings.

**Own any situation where you witness poor practice. Once you have decided something needs to be done do it. Don't leave it to someone else.**

### Being Non-Judgemental

Maintaining objectivity when you suspect poor practices can be challenging, as your instincts and perceptions have already alerted you to what seems like an uncomfortable situation.

Nevertheless, it's crucial to investigate your suspicions and for this reason, you should temporarily set aside any preconceived notions and attempt to conduct an unbiased observation.

This involves revisiting the situation with a completely open mindset.

**Being non-judgmental when witnessing what you suspect may be poor practice is essential for several reasons:**

### Objective Assessment:

To assess the situation accurately, you must approach it with an open and non-biased mindset.

Being non-judgmental allows you to focus on the facts and evidence rather than making assumptions or allowing personal opinions to cloud your judgment.

**Fair Treatment:**

Everyone deserves fair and impartial treatment, including those who may be involved in poor practice.

Jumping to conclusions or passing judgment prematurely can lead to unfair treatment or accusations based on assumptions rather than facts.

**Professionalism:**

Healthcare and social care professionals are expected to uphold high standards of professionalism and ethics.

Being non-judgmental demonstrates your commitment to these principles.

It shows that you are willing to give individuals involved in the situation the benefit of the doubt until all relevant information is gathered.

**Effective Communication:**

When addressing poor practice, effective communication is vital.

Being non-judgmental allows for more productive conversations with colleagues, superiors or those directly involved in the situation.

It fosters an environment where people are more likely to cooperate, share information and work toward resolving the issue.

**Avoiding Preconceived Biases:**

Preconceived biases or judgments can hinder your ability to see the full picture.

By setting aside preconceived notions and approaching the situation objectively, you are more likely to uncover the root causes of the issue and identify potential solutions.

**Preserving Professional Relationships:**

In healthcare and social care, professional relationships are crucial.

Being non-judgmental helps maintain trust and respect among colleagues and with the individuals receiving care.

It ensures that your actions are based on evidence and concern for their well-being rather than personal biases.

**Ethical Responsibility:**

Healthcare and social care professionals have an ethical responsibility to provide the best possible care and ensure the safety and well-being of those they serve.

Being non-judgmental aligns with this ethical duty by promoting fairness, transparency and a commitment to addressing concerns when they arise.

In summary, being non-judgmental is a fundamental aspect of addressing poor practice professionally and ethically.

It allows for objective assessment, fair treatment, effective communication and the preservation of professional relationships while fulfilling the ethical responsibility to ensure the highest quality of care and safety for individuals in healthcare and social care settings.

**Interpretation of the Situation**

Misunderstanding a situation can happen, so it's important to strive for as much certainty as possible regarding your interpretation of the situation.

Keeping detailed notes can assist in clarifying what you have witnessed or heard and these notes can also be valuable if you later decide to take further action.

If you have taken this step but still find yourself uncertain about the appropriate course of action, it is advisable to engage in a conversation with your supervisor.

- Communicate your concerns and what is troubling you

This conversation should help alleviate your worries, either by addressing your anxieties or by initiating a resolution process for the situation.

## Results of Not Dealing with Poor Practice

What is likely to happen if you do nothing?

- Nothing changes.
- Poor practice becomes embedded.
- Abuse or neglect takes place.

## Immediate Danger

In very serious situations when you think someone is in immediate danger:

- **You must report the incident immediately.**

## Noting Down What You have Witnessed or Heard

1. What have you seen or heard?
2. When did it happen?
3. What was the impact on the person being cared for?
4. Did you feel they were in danger of being immediately harmed or injured?
5. Is there anyone you check it out with?
6. If so, what was their response?

## 5 CHALLENGING IN THE MOMENT

Sometimes, when we come across something amiss in our workplace, we have the opportunity to immediately address the error in a non-confrontational manner.

This is commonly referred to as '**Challenging in the Moment**'.

For most individuals who have acted without careful consideration but without deliberate negligence, this kind of interaction should suffice to make them recognise the inappropriateness of their actions and encourage them to alter their behaviour or practice.

*As an example*, consider two co-workers who are aiding individuals during lunch but are engrossed in a conversation about their upcoming evening plans, not adequately engaging with the people they are assisting.

Addressing this situation could be as straightforward as saying:

*"Sarah, perhaps we can discuss your evening plans during the coffee break. Right now, let's focus on Michael. He might be signalling that he's finished eating. By the way, Michael's son paid her a visit yesterday and brought her a wonderful gift. You might want to ask her about it."*

**Why Challenge in the Moment?**

Delaying the response until a later time is ineffective

because the moment has passed and the caregiver will remain oblivious to their actions.

When confronted in a non-confrontational manner, a response is likely to be along the lines of:

*"I wasn't aware that I was behaving in that way".*

**Successful 'challenging in the moment'**

Making these types of challenges can be difficult and requires confidence.

To achieve positive outcomes, it's crucial to maintain respect and avoid patronising the individual you're addressing.

Practice these interactions with willing colleagues, family members or friends. This way, when you encounter a situation that requires immediate attention, you'll feel confident in addressing it.

**"Challenging in the moment" refers to addressing poor practice or issues as they occur and doing so effectively requires certain skills and approaches.**

**Here's more information on this:**

**Confidence:** Challenging in the moment can be intimidating, but confidence is key.

You need to believe in the importance of addressing the issue and have the self-assurance to do so professionally.

**Respect:** Maintaining respect is crucial.

Regardless of the situation, treating the individual involved with dignity and respect is essential.

Avoiding a patronising or confrontational tone is vital for productive communication.

**Practice:** Like any skill, addressing issues in the moment becomes easier with practice.

You can rehearse these interactions with colleagues, family members or friends.

This practice helps you become more comfortable with initiating difficult conversations.

### Sensitivity to the Situation:

Different situations may require different approaches.

Consider the context, the person involved and the severity of the issue.

Tailor your response accordingly.

For example, addressing an issue with a colleague may be handled differently than addressing an issue with a patient or client.

### Effective Communication:

Successful challenging in the moment relies on effective communication.

Be clear, concise and specific about the issue.

Use "I" statements to express your concerns and avoid making accusations.

For instance, say, "I feel uncomfortable about..." rather than "You're doing this wrong."

## Active Listening:

Encourage the other party to share their perspective. Actively listen to their response, as this can provide valuable insights into the situation.

It also demonstrates that you are open to understanding their point of view.

## Problem-Solving:

Focus on finding solutions rather than dwelling on the problem.

Offer suggestions for improvement or ask for their input on resolving the issue collaboratively.

## Emotional Regulation:

Stay composed and professional during challenging moments.

Emotional reactions can escalate the situation and hinder productive communication.

## Feedback Loop:

After addressing the issue, follow up to ensure that any agreed-upon changes are implemented and that the problem is resolved.

A feedback loop helps prevent the issue from recurring.

## Cultural Sensitivity:

Be mindful of cultural differences and communication styles.

What may be appropriate in one cultural context may not be in another.

**Remember that there's no one-size-fits-all approach, as it depends on the specific situation, your familiarity with the person you're addressing and your own personal communication style.**

Practice and experience will help refine your skills in challenging poor practice effectively.

The goal is to address issues promptly and professionally while maintaining the dignity and respect of all parties involved.

### Examples of how to challenge in the moment

**Direct Observation:** "Hey, Sarah, I noticed you were in a rush while assisting John with his meal. Let's take our time to ensure he's comfortable."

**Concern for Well-being:** "Is everything okay, David? You seem a bit distracted today. Sophie appeared a bit uneasy when..."

**Gentle Reminder:** "Oh, Maria, I think you might have forgotten to check on Robert's medication. I had a similar slip yesterday and it's crucial for his well-being."

**Maintaining Dignity:** "Lucy, I think we should give Jack some space for privacy during his personal care routine. He values his dignity and we should respect that."

**Empathy and Support:** "Jane, I understand it's been a challenging day, but let's ensure we provide emotional support to Emily. She seems a bit upset about..."

**Safety Concern:** "Mark, let's make sure we keep the area clear around Thomas's wheelchair. We want to prevent any accidents and ensure his safety."

**Effective Communication:** "Hey, Lisa, I noticed we were both on our phones during one-on-one time with Helen. Let's give her our full attention to encourage her engagement."

**Respect for Preferences:** "Tom, I know we have a schedule, but Emma prefers to do her exercises in the morning. Let's adapt to her preferences to make her more comfortable."

**Preserving Routine:** "Nina, I think we should stick to Sarah's usual routine for her meals. It helps her feel more in control of her day."

**Acknowledging Mistakes:** "John, I realised I forgot to bring George his favourite book yesterday. Let's make sure he has it today since it brings him so much comfort."

**Safety Concern:** "Emily, I noticed the side rail on Mr. Johnson's bed is down. Let's make sure it's up to prevent any falls and ensure his safety."

**Patient Comfort:** "Isabelle, I think Mrs. Rodriguez might need an extra blanket. She seems a bit cold and we want to keep her comfortable."

**Effective Communication:** "Michael, during our shift change, let's ensure we provide a thorough handover report about Mrs. Smith's condition and any changes."

**Medication Administration:** "Sarah, I believe we missed giving Mr. Patel his pain medication. Let's administer it now to manage his discomfort."

**Respect for Dignity:** "David, I noticed we didn't close the privacy curtain during Mr. Brown's examination. Let's ensure he has his privacy and maintains his dignity."

**Infection Control:** "Jessica, I think we should both wash our hands before attending to Mrs. Turner. Hand hygiene is crucial to prevent infections."

**Patient Engagement:** "John, I saw that Mrs. Davis was trying to reach her water bottle. Let's make sure it's within her reach so she can stay hydrated."

**Monitoring Vital Signs:** "Nurse, I noticed that Mr. Lee's oxygen levels are dropping. Can we check his oxygen supply and adjust it to keep him stable?"

**Mobility Support:** "Emma, I think we should assist Mr. Carter with his range of motion exercises today. It will help prevent stiffness and maintain his mobility."

**Nutrition and Hydration:** "James, I saw that Mrs. Garcia's meal tray is untouched. Let's check if there are any dietary preferences or issues preventing her from eating."

## USING MORE ASSERTIVE LANGUAGE

When you witness something potentially harmful (e.g. improper lifting and handling) there using more assertive language becomes necessary.

**Here are alternative phrases you could use:**

- "I'm quite uneasy about..."
- "I have significant concerns regarding..."
- "Please stop. This is causing distress."
- Using these expressions can effectively communicate your apprehension while encouraging corrective action

**If you see something that is very clearly abuse don't**

**challenge it but report it immediately.**

## ACTION TO TAKE IF 'CHALLENGING IN THE MOMENT' IS INEFFECTIVE

### Reporting

Addressing issues in the moment might prove ineffective. Despite your attempts, poor practice persists.

Alternatively, the situation you've come across may be of such gravity that addressing it directly is not the appropriate approach.

In such instances, it's essential to escalate the matter to your manager and draw their attention to the poor practice.

**When you report substandard work practices:**

- The manager is likely to conduct an observation of the individual's work and subsequently engage in a conversation with them.

- During this interaction, they may illustrate the correct procedures or organise training sessions to help the person improve their performance.

### Safeguarding

If the concern pertains to safeguarding, particularly if an individual under care has experienced abuse or is at risk, prompt action is imperative.

In such cases, it's crucial to report the situation without delay.

Your manager should take immediate steps by officially

notifying Adult and Local Services about the incident.

# 6 WHISTLEBLOWING

If you've already alerted your manager about poor practice but it **persists** without any **visible action** or if your manager is **directly involved** in the improper conduct:

- You must elevate your concerns to **higher levels within** your organisation.

This process is commonly referred to as **whistleblowing.**

Every healthcare and social care setting is mandated to establish a whistleblowing policy that offers guidance on when, why and how to engage in whistleblowing.

This policy should also outline the assistance and safeguards provided to individuals who 'blow the whistle'.

- Obtain a copy of your organisation's policy and use it as a resource to navigate the process.

Raising a concern, particularly through whistleblowing, can be a complex and emotionally charged process.

**Here's a closer look at the challenges, emotions and the duty of care involved:**

## Challenges:

**Fear of Retaliation:**

Whistleblowers often fear retaliation, such as job loss, demotion, harassment or damage to their professional reputation.

This fear can deter individuals from reporting concerns.

## Emotional Toll:

Whistleblowing can take an emotional toll on individuals.

It may lead to stress, anxiety or even depression, especially when they feel isolated or unsupported.

## Impact on Relationships:

Whistleblowing can strain relationships, both personal and professional.
Colleagues may view whistleblowers with suspicion or resentment, leading to workplace conflicts.

## Legal and Financial Risks:

Some individuals may be concerned about legal repercussions or financial consequences for themselves or their families.

# Emotions:

## Fear:

Fear is a common emotion when considering whistleblowing.

Fear of losing one's job, livelihood or reputation can be overwhelming.

## Anger and Frustration:

Whistleblowers may feel anger and frustration at witnessing wrongdoing or unethical behaviour.

These emotions can drive them to take action.
**Guilt:**

Some whistleblowers grapple with guilt, especially if they've been aware of an issue for a while before reporting it.

They may question whether they could have acted sooner.

**Isolation:**

Whistleblowers can feel isolated, as they may face backlash or ostracism from colleagues or peers who are loyal to the organisation.

**Relief:**

After reporting, there can be a sense of relief that they've taken action to address a concern and uphold their ethical values.

# Duty of Care:

In the context of whistleblowing, the duty of care is multifaceted:

**Duty to the Organisation:**

Whistleblowers often have a duty of loyalty to their organisation, but they also have a duty to uphold ethical standards and protect the welfare of others, including patients, clients or the public.

Duty to the Public:

When concerns involve public safety, healthcare professionals, for example, have a duty to protect the well-being of patients and clients.

Reporting concerns in such cases aligns with their ethical obligations.

**Duty to Self:**

Whistleblowers have a duty to safeguard their own well-being.

This includes addressing concerns about personal and professional repercussions.

Seeking legal counsel or support from advocacy groups can be part of this self-care.

**Duty to Transparency:**

Whistleblowers contribute to transparency and accountability in organisations and systems.

Their actions help identify and rectify issues that may otherwise go unaddressed, ultimately benefiting the public.

Balancing these duties can be **challenging**, but it's essential to recognise that the duty to protect public safety and uphold ethical standards often takes precedence.

**Whistleblowers play a vital role in holding organisations accountable and ensuring the well-being of those they serve.**

Adequate legal protections and support systems are crucial to help individuals fulfil their duty of care while minimising the emotional and professional toll of whistleblowing.

# Next Steps

When a health or social care worker blows the whistle using an organisation's policy and procedures, the organisation should follow a series of steps to address the concern appropriately.

**Here's what organisations should typically do:**

**Acknowledge Receipt:**

The organisation should acknowledge receipt of the whistleblower's concerns promptly.

This acknowledgment should include a timeline for the investigation process, which helps manage the whistleblower's expectations.

**Confidentiality:**

Maintain strict confidentiality throughout the process to protect the whistleblower's identity and prevent any potential retaliation.

**Appoint an Investigator:**

Designate a qualified and impartial investigator or investigation team to assess the concerns raised.

This person or team should have the necessary expertise and independence to conduct a thorough review.

**Investigation:**

Conduct a comprehensive investigation into the allegations.

This process may involve interviewing relevant parties, reviewing documentation and assessing the validity and severity of the concerns.

**Protection from Retaliation:**

Ensure that the whistleblower is protected from retaliation during and after the investigation.

This includes monitoring the work environment to prevent adverse actions against the whistleblower.

## Communication:

Keep the whistleblower informed about the progress of the investigation while respecting confidentiality.

Regular updates can help reduce anxiety and demonstrate the organisation's commitment to addressing the issue.

## Corrective Actions:

If the investigation substantiates the concerns, take appropriate corrective actions.

This may involve disciplinary measures for wrongdoers, changes in policies or procedures or other remedial actions to prevent further occurrences.

## Support for Whistleblower:

Provide support services to the whistleblower, including access to counselling, legal assistance or employee assistance programs.

Addressing the emotional and psychological well-being of the whistleblower is essential.

## Documentation:

Maintain thorough records of the investigation, including findings, actions taken and any changes to policies or procedures.

Proper documentation is critical for accountability and future reference.

**Report to Regulators:**

In some cases, organisations are legally required to report whistleblowing concerns to relevant regulatory bodies.

Compliance with reporting obligations is essential to ensure transparency and legal adherence.

**Preventing Future Occurrences:**

Use the lessons learned from the investigation to implement preventive measures and improve organisational practices.

This may involve training, policy revisions or enhanced monitoring.

**Feedback to Whistleblower:**

After the investigation is complete, provide feedback to the whistleblower on the outcomes and actions taken.

This communication helps close the loop and demonstrates the organisation's commitment to addressing the issue.

**Regular Reviews:**

Continuously monitor the effectiveness of the corrective actions and ensure that similar issues do not recur in the future.

Regular reviews and audits can help maintain accountability.

**Legal Protections:**

Ensure that the organisation complies with any legal

protections and anti-retaliation measures for whistleblowers as mandated by relevant laws and regulations.

Organisations should approach whistleblowing concerns with seriousness, transparency and a commitment to ethical conduct.

By following these steps, they can address poor practices, protect whistleblowers and improve overall accountability and patient/client safety.

## Care Quality Commission

Some individuals raise concerns externally to the regulatory body (Care Quality Commission (CQC)).

The CQC provides a section on their website for anonymous reporting.

You should consider taking this step only if you have concerns that your employer:

- 
- Will conceal the issue
- Will treat you unfairly in response to your complaint
- Has not resolved the matter despite your prior communication with them

An employee cannot be terminated due to whistleblowing, provided they genuinely believe that their disclosure serves the public interest and meets one of the following conditions:

- When someone's health and safety is at risk
- In cases of environmental harm
- When a criminal offence has occurred
- If the company is in violation of the law, such as lacking proper insurance
- When someone is concealing unethical actions

# 7 RESOURCES FOR CHALLENGING POOR PRACTICE

Challenging poor practice in healthcare and social care requires access to resources and support.

Here are some key resources that can be helpful:

**Organisational Policies and Procedures:**

Most healthcare and social care organisations have policies and procedures in place for addressing and reporting poor practice.

These documents outline the steps to follow when concerns arise.

Familiarise yourself with your organisation's policies.

**Training and Education:**

Training programs and courses on ethics, patient safety and professional conduct are valuable resources.

They can help individuals understand what constitutes poor practice and how to address it effectively.

**Colleague Support:**

Peer support can be invaluable when challenging poor practice.

Discussing concerns with colleagues can provide different perspectives and guidance on how to handle specific situations.

**Supervisors and Managers:**

Supervisors and managers play a crucial role in addressing poor practice.

They can provide guidance, support and escalation paths when necessary.

**Whistleblowing Hotlines:**

Some organisations have anonymous reporting mechanisms or hotlines that allow employees to report concerns confidentially.

These can be a safe way to report poor practice when you fear retaliation.

**Professional Organisations:**

Healthcare and social care professionals often belong to associations or organisations related to their field.

These organisations may offer resources, guidelines and ethical frameworks for addressing poor practice.

**Regulatory Bodies:**

Regulatory bodies and government agencies oversee healthcare and social care services.

They may have guidelines and reporting mechanisms for addressing poor practice.

In the UK, for example, you can contact organisations like the Care Quality Commission (CQC) or the Nursing and Midwifery Council (NMC) for guidance.

**Legal and Ethical Frameworks:**

Familiarise yourself with the legal and ethical frameworks that apply to your profession.

These frameworks often provide guidance on professional conduct and the reporting of poor practice.

**Patient Advocacy Groups:**

Some patient advocacy groups provide resources and support for individuals who have experienced poor practice.

They can offer guidance on how to seek resolution and justice.

**Counselling and Support Services:**

Challenging poor practice can be emotionally challenging.

Access to counselling and support services, either through your organisation or independently, can help you cope with the stress and emotional toll.

**Books and Publications:**

There are many books, articles and publications that address ethics, patient safety and addressing poor practice in healthcare and social care.

These can provide valuable insights and strategies.

**Online Forums and Communities:**

Online forums and communities related to healthcare and social care can be platforms for discussing challenges, seeking advice and connecting with peers facing similar situations (maintaining patient/client confidentiality).

**Legal Advice:**

In cases where poor practice involves legal issues, seeking legal advice from qualified professionals is essential to understand your rights and options.

Remember that the availability of these resources may vary by location and profession.

It's important to proactively seek out the resources that are most relevant to your situation and needs when addressing poor practice.

# 8 REFLECTION

Reflection plays a significant role after challenging poor practice or when contemplating doing so.

It serves several important purposes:

**Learning and Self-Improvement:**

Reflection allows healthcare and social care professionals to review their actions and decisions.

They can consider what went well, what could have been done differently and what lessons can be learned from the experience.

This process supports ongoing professional development and continuous improvement.

**Emotional Processing:**

Challenging poor practice can be emotionally taxing.

Reflection provides a space to process and manage the emotions associated with confronting colleagues, supervisors or systemic issues.

It helps individuals make sense of their feelings and reactions.

## Decision Evaluation:

Healthcare professionals often need to make rapid decisions when challenging poor practice.

Reflecting afterward allows them to evaluate whether their actions were appropriate and effective.

It helps them assess whether further steps or alternative approaches are needed.

### Identification of Systemic Issues:

Poor practice isn't always an isolated incident.

Reflecting on a specific instance of poor practice may reveal systemic issues within the organisation or healthcare system.

Identifying these issues is crucial for advocating for broader changes.

### Supporting Ethical Practice:

Reflection reinforces the commitment to ethical practice.

It helps professionals reaffirm their dedication to providing safe, compassionate and patient-centred care.

It also assists in aligning actions with ethical principles.

### Building Resilience:

Challenging poor practice can be challenging and sometimes met with resistance or backlash.

Reflecting on past experiences and identifying strategies for improvement can build resilience, helping professionals approach similar situations more confidently in the future.

**Enhancing Communication:**

Reflection can improve communication skills.

Professionals can consider how they communicated their concerns and whether their message was received as intended.

This insight can guide better communication in future challenges.

**Promoting Accountability:**

Reflecting on the outcomes of challenging poor practice reinforces the importance of accountability.

It reminds professionals that they have a duty to report and address concerns to prevent future harm.

**Supporting Decision-Making:**

Reflection provides a foundation for making informed decisions about whether to escalate concerns, seek further guidance or pursue additional actions.

It helps professionals weigh the potential risks and benefits.

**Documentation:**

In some cases, reflection involves documenting the details of the challenge and the response.

This documentation can be valuable if further actions, such as reporting to regulatory bodies or legal authorities, become necessary.

Overall, reflection is a critical component of the professional practice of healthcare and social care.

It promotes ethical conduct, supports learning and improvement and ensures that individuals are better prepared to address poor practice effectively in the future.

It should be integrated into the ongoing practice of all healthcare and social care professionals.

## ABOUT THE AUTHOR

Susan Rogers, HSC Training Link has been developing resources for the health and social care sector since 2004.

In addition to books, HSC Training Link has a range of training and teaching resources available on:

www.healthandsocialcareresources.co.uk

www.ingramcontent.com/pod-product-compliance
Lightning Source LLC
Chambersburg PA
CBHW062355290526
45794CB00005B/2229